Original title:

Misty Echoes Amid the Fae Cup

Author: Sabrina Sarvik

ISBN HARDBACK: 978-1-80562-059-4

ISBN PAPERBACK: 978-1-80563-580-2

# The Flicker of Faery's Breath

In twilight's glow, the faeries dance,
With wings that shimmer, a fleeting glance.
They weave through shadows, soft and light,
In the hush of evening, taking flight.

They beckon dreams from hidden streams,
And whisper secrets, woven themes.
A flicker here, a giggle there,
Their laughter lingers in scented air.

Beneath the stars, they spin their spells,
In ancient woods where magic dwells.
A journey whispered on the breeze,
Through lilac fields and tangled trees.

The moonlit path, their shimmering thread,
Where wishes scatter, unspoken, bred.
In faery's breath, the world transforms,
In silken veils, the calm conforms.

So close your eyes, let visions flow,
In every breeze, let wonder grow.
The flicker of faery, soft and bright,
Invites us into the magic's light.

## Timeless Journeys in Enchanted Fields

In fields of gold where wildflowers sway,
Eternal journeys weave and play.
Each bloom a story, a moment caught,
In nature's art, enchantment wrought.

With every step, the path unfolds,
A tapestry woven in timeless folds.
The rustle of leaves, a gentle guide,
Invites the heart to walk alongside.

Barefoot on earth, with hands outstretched,
Grasping the sunlight, soft and etched.
Through valleys deep and mountains high,
Adventure beckons, beneath the sky.

In enchanted realms where spirits sing,
The whispers of hope in breezes cling.
Each cloud that drifts, a canvas vast,
In the dance of futures, present, past.

So gather your dreams, let courage swell,
In enchanted fields where stories dwell.
For every journey, a spark ignites,
Timeless in wonder, endless in sights.

## Starlit Conversations with Nature's Spirits

In the velvet night when shadows creep,
The spirits of nature begin to speak.
With shimmering stardust, they paint the air,
In echoes of whispers, dreams laid bare.

The murmurs of rivers, soft and low,
Converse with the moon in a gentle flow.
Crickets strum their symphony bright,
In harmony woven with silver light.

Beneath ancient trees, secrets unfold,
As stories of ages are lovingly told.
The breeze carries laughter of creatures unseen,
As starlight bathes the landscape serene.

Every rustle, each flutter, a message divine,
Tales spun from silk on a shimmering line.
In conversations laced with the night's refrain,
Nature's spirits remind us, we are the same.

So pause for a moment, and listen near,
In starlit conversations, the magic is clear.
For in every whisper, every sigh,
Nature's heart beats, and we learn to fly.

# The Allure of the Whispering Boughs


In wooded groves where whispers play,
The boughs of trees have much to say.
With every sway, a secret shared,
In nature's bosom, souls laid bare.

The ancient trunks, with wisdom deep,
Hold stories sung, too rich to keep.
Beneath their shade, in gentle arcs,
We find our dreams, igniting sparks.

Leaves like laughter in the breeze,
Painting colors that dance with ease.
In tangled roots where fairies hide,
The allure beckons, our hearts abide.

Each rustling branch, like fingers trace,
The ebb and flow of time and space.
In the whispers sweet, we lose our fear,
As magic swirls in the atmosphere.

So linger long beneath their grace,
And let the boughs embrace your place.
For in their chorus, truth lies deep,
The allure of whispers, secrets we keep.

# Murmurs of Timeless Elegance

In whispers soft, the ancient trees,
Their boughs adorned with golden leaves.
They tell of dreams lost to the night,
And secrets cloaked in silver light.

Through twisted roots and mossy stones,
Echoes dance in hushed tones.
With every breath, the past unfolds,
In stories woven, rich with gold.

The moonlight weaves a gentle spell,
As nightingale sings in distant dell.
The stars, like gems in velvet sea,
Gaze down on hearts that long to be.

In shadows deep, where wonders hide,
The echoes of our souls reside.
Each sigh entwined with crisp night air,
A fleeting touch, forever rare.

In twilight's arms, we find our place,
A quiet pause, a fleeting grace.
Murmurs drift as time takes flight,
In elegance born of starry night.

## The Fae's Embrace of the Forgotten Glade

In whispers brushed by silver dew,
Where fae flit softly, hidden from view.
The glade awakes with laughter sweet,
As ancient magic stirs in beat.

Amidst the blooms of vibrant hue,
The fae spin dreams the twilight knew.
Their dances weave through whispering grass,
In moments caught, like glimmers of glass.

Beneath a canopy of emerald leaves,
The heart of nature gently heaves.
A world alive with shadows bright,
In sacred realms kissed by starlight.

With every step, a spell is cast,
Echoes of joy from ages past.
In every rustle, every sigh,
The fae's embrace, a lullaby.

Forgotten paths lead to the light,
Where daylight fades, and dreams take flight.
In whispers soft, the magic stays,
In the glade's embrace, where wonder plays.

# Reflections on the Silvered Brook

Upon the bank where waters gleam,
A tranquil flow, like whispered dream.
The silver brook, in moon's embrace,
Holds secrets deep, a silent place.

With every ripple, stories flow,
Of ancient tides and lands below.
The stars reflect in crystal waves,
A dance of light, where shadow braves.

Beneath the willows, soft and low,
The gentle breeze begins to blow.
Each sigh of night enfolds the calm,
As nature hums her soothing psalm.

And as I gaze, the visions spark,
Of journeys taken through the dark.
The brook, a mirror to my mind,
In every current, truths I find.

So let my thoughts, like waters, roam,
In twilight's hush, they'll find their home.
Reflections whisper of what's true,
In silvered streams that call for you.

# Veiled Journeys Through the Twilight

In twilight's cloak, where shadows blend,
Paths carved by time, they twist and bend.
With every step, a world concealed,
In veils of dusk, the heart is healed.

The whispering winds weave tales of yore,
Of ancient realms and distant shore.
With every footfall on the ground,
A symphony of dreams is found.

Amidst the mists, a lantern speaks,
Guiding souls through hidden peaks.
In echoes soft, the past will sing,
Of love and loss, of every thing.

The night unveils its velvet charm,
Embracing all with tender calm.
In twilight's dance, secrets unfold,
Every path rich with stories told.

So take my hand, let's venture wide,
Through veiled journeys, side by side.
In twilight's grasp, let's lose the day,
And find the magic in the sway.

# Fragments of Moonlight's Breath

In the stillness of the night,
Whispers shape the silver light.
Stars adorn the velvet skies,
As dreams take flight on whispered sighs.

Shadows dance on ancient trees,
Where secrets float upon the breeze.
Earth and sky in soft embrace,
Hold the echoes of a trace.

Moonbeams weave through quiet glades,
Casting charms where silence wades.
Each glimmer tells a tale untold,
Of hearts entwined and fates behold.

Beneath the glow, the world awaits,
For magic stirs as night abates.
With every breath, the night unfolds,
The universe in dreams enfolds.

In fragments caught on twilight's breath,
A promise born beyond the death.
We wander through this mystic air,
To find the moonlight's secrets rare.

## Sprites' Serenade at Dusk

As twilight falls, the songbirds call,
In shades of gold, the shadows sprawl.
Sprites gather 'neath the willow's sway,
To sing of dusk, the end of day.

Gentle laughter fills the air,
With twinkling eyes, they dance in pairs.
Soft melodies, like threads of silk,
They spin a tapestry with milk.

Among the blooms, they prance and twirl,
With every note, their wings unfurl.
A serenade so sweetly sung,
Among the blooms, forever young.

The brook hums in a soothing tone,
As shadows stretch, the night is grown.
Stars begin to dot the skies,
While sprites weave dreams with lullabies.

And as the moon begins to rise,
Their laughter drifts through velvet skies.
In this moment, hearts unite,
With sprites' serenade, pure and light.

# Veils of Enchantment Unfurled

In the dawn's soft, tender grace,
Veils of magic start to trace.
Colors blend in gentle hues,
Awakening the morning muse.

Whispers float on golden air,
Every promise laced with care.
With each glance, the world transforms,
In harmony, the heart conforms.

Dreams are woven in the light,
As shadows dance, taking flight.
On silken threads, the wonders twirl,
Enchantment flows, a living pearl.

The forest hums a song of old,
Where stories whispered, brave and bold.
Each leaf a tome of wisdom shared,
In veils of magic, hearts are bared.

As dawn unfolds its tender arms,
We find ourselves in nature's charms.
With every step, new worlds await,
In veils of enchantment, love's estate.

# A Woven Tapestry of Time

Every thread a life's embrace,
Woven tightly, spun with grace.
Moments captured, bright and dark,
In the fabric, each soul's spark.

Time unfurls in vibrant hues,
With tales of joy and bittersweet blues.
Each stitch a breath, a tale revealed,
In the tapestry our fates are healed.

The weaver's hands, though worn and weak,
Hold the stories we dare not speak.
In gentle folds, we find our place,
Each heart a thread, love's trace of grace.

Through winding paths and endless streams,
Time dances on with woven dreams.
Each encounter, a fateful design,
In the cradle of moments divine.

As the pattern of life unwinds,
We cherish all it intertwines.
In this art, we find the rhyme,
Within a woven tapestry of time.

# The Echoing Call of Enchanted Woods

In the heart of the forest deep,
Where ancient secrets often sleep,
Echoes whisper through the leaves,
Tales of magic the wood believes.

Moonlight dances on the glade,
Casting shadows, a mystic shade,
Footsteps tread on paths untold,
In this realm where dreams unfold.

Creatures stir with twilight's breath,
Guardians of the woods, in depth,
They beckon softly, hear their song,
A calling where enchanted belong.

Amidst the ferns and tangled vines,
Where timeless beauty intertwines,
The echoing call grows faint yet near,
A melody only the brave can hear.

So come, brave heart, and heed the sound,
In enchanted woods, lost hopes are found,
For within the echo lies your fate,
A journey begun at destiny's gate.

# Flickers of Light in the Gloom

When shadows gather, dim and cold,
Flickers of light, stories unfold,
In the gloom, where fears may creep,
Hope ignites, its promise to keep.

Lanterns swing on gentle breeze,
Casting warmth through ancient trees,
Each glow a beacon, bright and true,
Guiding spirits, old and new.

Through the mist, the fire flies,
Dancing 'neath the starlit skies,
They weave a tapestry so fine,
A path through darkness, divine design.

In the hush of night, they play,
Chasing every fear away,
With laughter sweet as morning dew,
They brighten all, both me and you.

Hold on tight to flickering spells,
In your heart, the magic dwells,
For even in the darkest night,
There lies the chance for wondrous light.

# Whims of the Wind and Whispers

The wind it sings, a playful tune,
Whisking softly past the moon,
Carrying secrets on fond sighs,
Beneath the vast, enchanted skies.

Whispers float through fields of gold,
Tales of love and legends bold,
In every gust, a story's spun,
Unraveling beneath the sun.

Through the valleys, wild and free,
Whims take flight like birds at sea,
They rustle through the leaves and branches,
A dance of life, full of chances.

In the twilight, when stillness reigns,
Listen closely, hear the plains,
For every whisper, every whim,
Holds a world that beckons him.

So chase the wind and heed the call,
For in its laughter, we find it all,
In every whisper, let dreams unfurl,
A timeless magic in this world.

# The Fairies' Hidden Haven

In a glen where sunlight streams,
Lie hidden paths of whispered dreams,
Fairies flit on gossamer wings,
Guardians of the joy they bring.

Their laughter bubbles like a brook,
In every shadowed nook and crook,
With shimmering dust in the air,
They weave enchantments everywhere.

Among the flowers, soft and bright,
In petals kissed by morning light,
They dance beneath an azure dome,
Creating magic, calling home.

But tread with care on twilight's edge,
Where veils of mist form nature's pledge,
For here, the fairies gently play,
And weave the threads of night and day.

To find the haven, pure and true,
You must believe in fairies too,
For only those with open hearts,
Will see the world where magic starts.

# Revelry in the Sorcery of Twilight

In twilight's hush, the spells unwind,
Where whispers weave and secrets bind.
A flicker of light, a shimmer of glee,
Magic ignites in all that we see.

Beneath the stars, the creatures prance,
In moonlit glades, they twirl and dance.
With laughter soft, the night is spun,
In revelry shared, our hearts are one.

The cauldron bubbles, aromas rise,
As fairy lights dot the velvet skies.
With every sip, the world transforms,
In twilight's embrace, true magic warms.

Against the dusk, a shadow looms,
Yet courage blooms amidst the glooms.
With every heartbeat, the air grows bright,
We revel together in the magic of night.

So raise your glasses, toast the air,
To wonders found and dreams laid bare.
For in this moment, we dare to soar,
In twilight's magic, forevermore.

# Reflections of an Otherworldly Night

Stars waltz high in a velvet sea,
Echoes of dreams call out to me.
Each twinkle whispers of realms untold,
In the night's embrace, our souls unfold.

Moonlight bathes the world in silver,
Spectres dance, and shadows quiver.
With secrets spun in the misty air,
I feel the pulse of magic rare.

The nightingale sings a haunting tune,
Glimmers of fate beneath the moon.
Through tangled paths, my heart takes flight,
In otherworldly dreams of the night.

Reflections ripple on the still pond,
A bridge to the places we dream beyond.
With every heartbeat, the cosmos calls,
Enchanted whispers as night gently falls.

As dawn approaches, shadows blend,
In this twilight pact, our spirits mend.
For in this realm where magic reigns,
Lie unspoken truths and ancient chains.

# The Celestial Dance of the Lost

Through starlit paths, the lost ones roam,
In cosmic ballets, they search for home.
With every turn, the galaxies spin,
In the dance of fate, new journeys begin.

Their laughter echoes through the vast unknown,
In constellations, their stories are sown.
With twinkling eyes, they forge their way,
In the celestial ballet where hopes will sway.

Veils of stardust shimmer bright,
Guiding lost souls in the still of night.
With every step, the universe swells,
In the rhythm of time, a spell it compels.

Spirits collide in a radiant frame,
Adrift in a dream, they call each name.
As the cosmos twirls in a dance divine,
In the heart of the night, their paths align.

So let their stories paint the skies,
With hues of hope and cosmic ties.
In the celestial dance, they find their grace,
In the embrace of stars, they find their place.

# Tales from the Enchanted Thicket

In the heart of the woods, where magic lies,
Whispers of old weave 'neath the skies.
With ancients watching from branches high,
The tales of the thicket breathe and sigh.

Each leaf a story, each shadow a song,
In the enchanted realm where we all belong.
With gnarled roots that stretch through time,
The pulse of the forest is a timeless rhyme.

Creatures of wonder slip through the haze,
In a waltz with fate that forever stays.
With every rustle, adventures unfurl,
In the thicket's embrace, the magic swirls.

Fables of courage and friendship bloom,
As lanterns flicker in the lingering gloom.
With secrets shared beneath the moon's glow,
In the thicket's heart, our spirits flow.

So gather 'round with stories to share,
Of mystical journeys, of love and care.
For in this thicket where wonders combine,
We find the magic that forever shines.

# Elfin Laughter in the Dew

In the morning's gentle light,
Elves dance through fields of green,
Their laughter echoes, soft and bright,
Spreading joy where none have seen.

Dewdrops shimmer on the grass,
Like diamonds kissed by dawn,
With every twirl, the wildflowers pass,
In a world where time goes on.

Whispers ride the morning breeze,
As petals sway with grace,
In every rustle of the leaves,
Elves find their secret place.

They weave enchantments, tales untold,
In the midst of nature's play,
With giggles bright and hearts so bold,
They chase dull worries away.

So linger near, and listen well,
To laughter ringing clear,
In morning dew, where magic dwells,
Each moment's hope draws near.

## Beneath the Starlit Canopy

Underneath the starry skies,
Where night's cloak wraps the earth,
Dreams flutter by like fireflies,
In the silence, find your worth.

Whispers drift upon the air,
Stories shimmer in the night,
Each twinkling spark, a wish laid bare,
Guiding hearts to pure delight.

The moon dangles high and bright,
Casting silver o'er the land,
Awakening the deep of night,
As darkness gives a gentle hand.

In the quiet, shadows roam,
While echoes of the world remain,
In this space, we find our home,
Where dreams and reality entertain.

So breathe in deep, and let it flow,
The magic that the night unfolds,
Beneath this sky, we come to know,
A tapestry of dreams retold.

# Hushed Murmurs by the Glimmering Stream

By the banks where waters flow,
Hushed whispers tell the tale,
Of wanderers long ago,
Their paths marked by the pale.

Moonlit ripples kiss the stones,
In rhythms soft and kind,
Each secret shared, each heart atones,
As peace is left behind.

The trees lend ears to every sound,
Glimmers dance upon the wave,
In the quiet, comfort found,
With nature, gentle and brave.

Time meanders like the brook,
With stories waiting to unwind,
In every nook and every crook,
A world of wonder intertwined.

So come, dear friend, and softly sit,
Let murmurs fill your soul,
With every drop, your worries flit,
As the stream plays its role.

# A Chalice of Dreams and Dust

In a chalice made of glass,
Lay dreams gathered from afar,
With every sip, the moments pass,
Sparkling like a distant star.

Dust of ages, rich and fine,
Swirls within the gentle drink,
Each drop a whisper, so divine,
Unlocks the heart that dares to think.

With every taste, the tales revive,
Of magic held in each embrace,
In this place where dreams survive,
Hope glimmers in every trace.

Embrace the night, allow the flow,
Let time bend as dreams collide,
Within this cup, the worlds bestow,
All wishes buried deep inside.

So raise your glass, and toast the night,
To moments shared and treasures found,
In a chalice glowing bright,
May dreams and dust forever sound.

# Glade of the Enchanted Hollow

In the glade where whispers dwell,
The moonlight casts its wondrous spell.
Leaves dance softly in the night,
As dreams awaken in pure delight.

Mossy stones and ancient trees,
Carry tales upon the breeze.
Fairy echoes touch the air,
A symphony beyond compare.

Starlit paths and secret streams,
Guide the wanderer's wild dreams.
With every step, a magic found,
In this hollow, joy abounds.

Creatures small and spirits grand,
Join together, hand in hand.
Harmony in every tone,
In this haven they call home.

So linger long and breathe it in,
Where the magic never dims.
In the glade, your heart will see,
The enchantment meant to be.

## Sylvan Serenades of the Night


In the forest, shadows sway,
As nightingale begins to play.
Softly strumming on a breeze,
Nature sings beneath the trees.

Crickets chirp a gentle tune,
While fireflies join the moon.
Twinkling lights in nighttime dance,
Every flicker, a secret chance.

Whispers flutter through the leaves,
As the world gently believes.
In this twilight, dreams take flight,
Sylvan serenades of night.

Echoes of the twilight choir,
Kindle soft a hidden fire.
In every note that fills the air,
Lies the magic everywhere.

So close your eyes and fade away,
Let the melodies gently sway.
In the night, you'll find your heart,
In the music, a brand new start.

# A Dance of Light and Shadows

In the twilight's soft embrace,
Light and shadows dance with grace.
A waltz of dreams in endless play,
Guiding hearts at close of day.

Flickering candles, shadows gleam,
Illuminating every dream.
As the stars begin to hum,
Underneath, the night feels fun.

The trees sway lightly in the breeze,
Harboring secrets among the leaves.
Every flicker, a story told,
In twilight's warmth, all hearts unfold.

A tapestry of dark and light,
Weaves together the starry night.
In the silence, magic grows,
In the dance, pure love bestows.

So hold your breath and take a chance,
Join the world in this great dance.
For in shadows, hearts align,
In the light, our souls entwine.

## The Hidden Path to Arcane Realms

Beneath the boughs where magic stirs,
A path awaits, through ferns and spurs.
Twilight beckons with whispered calls,
To secret realms behind the walls.

Winding trails of silver mist,
Await those brave enough to risk.
With every step, old echoes ring,
As ancient lore begins to sing.

Adventurers fair with questing hearts,
Seek the world where wonder starts.
A flicker glows, the journey's near,
In the shadows, fate draws near.

Veils of mystery gently part,
Unveiling truths that stir the heart.
In hidden realms where spirits dwell,
Time stands still, and magic's swell.

So gather courage, heed the call,
The hidden path invites us all.
In arcane realms, our spirits soar,
Discovering what lies in store.

# Whispers of the Hidden Glen

In the glen where shadows weave,
Softly whisper tales they leave,
Secrets held in twilight's breath,
Wrapped in magic, life and death.

A brook babbles ancient lore,
Through mossy stones, forevermore,
Trees stand guard, with leaves like gold,
Their stories waiting to be told.

Beneath the boughs, a world awaits,
Where fate and fortune gently mate,
A flick'ring path that leads us near,
To dreams awakened, bright and clear.

In shadows where the fairies tread,
And petals fall like whispered threads,
Each footstep sings a wild refrain,
In harmony with softest rain.

So linger long and breathe it in,
The magic hum that brews within,
For in the glen, hearts intertwine,
With every breath, the stars align.

# Enchantment in the Dewlit Grove

In the grove where daylight fades,
Magic lingers in cool glades,
Dewdrops glisten on each leaf,
Holding secrets like a thief.

With every breeze, a whisper calls,
Echoes dance along the walls,
Of ancient trees with twisted roots,
Guarding tales of hidden fruits.

The air is thick with fragrant blooms,
While twilight weaves its shadowed loom,
Creating spells on every branch,
Where starlight gleams and crickets dance.

Beneath the arch of leafy skies,
The night unfolds its sweet surprise,
With every rustle, every sigh,
Enchantments spark as time drifts by.

So wander deep, let wonders flow,
In dewlits' embrace, let spirits grow,
For in this grove, magic resides,
And binds us close with nature's tides.

# Reflections in the Moonlit Moss

When night descends on velvet skies,
And silver light softly lies,
The moss wears shadows, rich and deep,
A cradle where the dreamers sleep.

Each glimmer holds a flick'ring tale,
Of wishes whispered in the pale,
A dance of dreams that come alive,
As moonbeams weave and shadows thrive.

The forest sighs beneath the glow,
A tranquil heart where secrets flow,
Rippling like the gentle tide,
In every nook where magic hides.

Reflections dance on mossy beds,
Where starlight whispers, lightly treads,
Inviting us to lend an ear,
To all the wonders drawing near.

So walk with care on nature's floor,
And find the tales that dreamers bore,
For in this moonlit, mossy space,
Our hearts will find a sacred place.

## Secrets Beneath the Canopy Veil

In the depths of emerald shade,
Whispers float like gentle jade,
The canopy hides secrets old,
In every branch, a story told.

Sunbeams pierce the flora thick,
Dancing wildly, quick and quick,
With every leaf that bends and sways,
A shiver sings of ancient ways.

The air is filled with magic's hum,
A soft invitation to succumb,
To wonders wrapped in emerald grace,
In nature's warm, embracing space.

Beneath the veil where shadows drift,
A tapestry of dreams can lift,
To realms unseen by weary eyes,
Where every heartbeat softly lies.

So heed the call, let spirits soar,
Discover secrets, evermore,
For in this sacred, shaded trail,
Life unfolds beneath the veil.

# The Whispered Dance of Sylvan Beings

In twilight's haze, the shadows weave,
Where ancient trees hold secrets deep,
The sylvan dance begins to breathe,
A soft enchantment lulls to sleep.

With silken steps beneath the moon,
They twirl and sing in muffled tones,
Their laughter echoes, faint but soon,
A symphony of whispered groans.

The leaves applaud each graceful spin,
As fireflies spark like stars in flight,
They gather close, where dreams begin,
And share their warmth throughout the night.

In shimmering glades, the magic bends,
Where time flows free and worries cease,
These gentle souls, our truest friends,
Invite us to their world of peace.

So linger not in daylight's glare,
But venture forth to find your place,
In whispered dances, light as air,
The sylvan beings leave their trace.

# Luminescent Revelations in the Quiet Grove

In quiet groves where shadows play,
A glow arises through the leaves,
Illuminating hidden ways,
Where spirit whispers softly weaves.

Each glimmer holds a tale untold,
Of journeys past and dreams anew,
In every spark, a truth unfolds,
As light reveals what once we knew.

The forest breathes, a sacred hymn,
As luminescent paths invite,
With every step, the shadows swim,
Embraced by warmth of soft moonlight.

Beneath the boughs, the secrets bloom,
In gentle laughter, joy ignites,
The night enfolds a velvet room,
Where stars align with whirls of light.

So venture forth where magic thrives,
And let the glow guide you to see,
In quiet groves, our spirit dives,
To grasp the wonders yet to be.

# Echoes of Forgotten Truths in the Breeze

Amidst the whispers of the trees,
The breeze reveals long-lost delights,
In rustling leaves, the ancient keys,
To secrets held in starry nights.

Each sigh of wind brings tales of old,
Of journeys taken, loves once known,
In echoes soft, their stories told,
Through cradled whispers, seeds are sown.

With every gust, the memories swell,
In patterns woven, time transcends,
For in the air, the heart can tell,
The truth that lies in dreams and bends.

So listen close to nature's song,
For every breeze holds wisdom's grace,
In nature's arms, we all belong,
To find our truth in this embrace.

As twilight fades and stars arise,
The echoes weave through space and time,
With every breath, behold the prize,
The whispered heartbeats, pure and prime.

# Twilight's Embrace of Nature's Mystique

Amidst the trees, shadows bend,
Whispers of secrets, nature's friend.
Crimson hues in the fading light,
A world awaits, cloaked in night.

Gentle breezes sing through leaves,
Starlit paths where the heart believes.
Mysterious creatures flicker and dart,
In twilight's realm, magic shall start.

The moon ascends with a watchful eye,
Casting dreams in the velvet sky.
Every blossom begins to hum,
In nature's arms, we're never numb.

Echoes of laughter in the glen,
Draw us closer, time and again.
Twilight weaves its soft embrace,
In nature's dance, we find our place.

Our spirits rise as shadows play,
In this enchanted, fleeting ballet.
Together we stand, as the stars align,
In twilight's embrace, our hearts entwine.

# Chronicles of Twinkling Skies

In the stillness, stars do gleam,
Woven tales in a midnight dream.
Each sparkle holds a story bright,
Chronicles birthed in the long, dark night.

The whispers of comets, swift and free,
Speak of adventures beyond the sea.
An ancient song floats on the breeze,
Of forgotten lands and timeless peas.

Planets dance in a cosmic waltz,
Painting the sky with silver vaults.
Galaxy trails, like brushstrokes wide,
In this cosmic canvas, we confide.

Nights unfold with a gentle sigh,
As constellations write their reply.
Maps of wonder etched in light,
In the twinkling skies, hearts take flight.

In each moment, a story spun,
Under the gaze of the setting sun.
In the tapestry of time, we find,
Chronicles of the stars intertwined.

# Ethereal Melodies by the Moonlit Shore

Whispers of waves in a soft caress,
Lullabies sung in the night's duress.
Moonbeams dance on the ocean's sway,
Ethereal notes dream the night away.

Shells gather stories of ages past,
Each echo a memory, steadfast.
The breeze carries songs of the sea,
In moonlit realms, we long to be.

Drifting melodies rise and fall,
In harmony's cradle, we find our call.
With every splash against the sand,
A symphony plays, so close at hand.

The nightingale joins in sweet refrain,
To serenade the soft, sweet pain.
As stars twinkle in playful mirth,
We lose ourselves in this gentle birth.

By the shore, where spirits glean,
Ethereal threads bind each unseen.
Together we sail on dreams so pure,
With melodies that forever endure.

# The Guardian of the Shimmering Grove

In a grove where the silver leaves sway,
A guardian whispers the end of day.
With watchful eyes, timeless and deep,
In this haven, secrets keep.

Ancient roots weave stories untold,
Beneath the boughs of the brave and bold.
Flickering lights through the branches weave,
In the shimmering grove, we believe.

Echoes of laughter bounce off bark,
In this sanctuary, magic sparks.
Every creature bows in respect,
To the guardian, wise and perfect.

With each dusk, a promise unfurls,
As twilight descends, the mystery swirls.
Together we tread on this sacred ground,
Where harmony's whispers are truly profound.

In the heart of the grove, peace resides,
With the guardian's love as our guide.
In the shimmering shadows, we find our way,
In nature's arms, come what may.

# Celestial Echoes in the Enchanted Wilds

In twilight's glow where shadows blend,
The whispers dance on winds that bend.
A silver moon, with watchful eye,
Awakens dreams that dare to fly.

Among the trees where secrets lay,
The stars align, as night meets day.
Each rustling leaf tells tales of old,
Of paths forgotten, brave and bold.

With every step, the magic stirs,
In hidden nooks, new worlds occur.
A symphony of heartbeats found,
In echoes soft, the wild resounds.

The fireflies weave a tapestry bright,
Guiding wanderers through the night.
A call from deep within the glade,
Where hopes and dreams have never stayed.

So come and roam the wilds anew,
Where every glance reveals a clue.
Embrace the wonder, let it grow,
In enchanted woods where starlight flows.

# Fluttering Secrets Beneath the Silvery Bough

In verdant realms where whispers sigh,
The secrets flutter, low and high.
Beneath the boughs that arch with grace,
A hidden world begins to trace.

With every breeze, the leaves will share,
The tales of creatures that once dared.
A dance of light in shadows played,
An ancient bond, now gently laid.

The dewdrops kiss the morning air,
While gentle dreams weave everywhere.
In every petal, every bloom,
A hint of magic starts to loom.

Through tangled roots, the stories creep,
In whispered tones, they softly leap.
A journey waits for hearts to gain,
In silence rich, where joy remains.

So wander forth, embrace the calm,
Where every breath becomes a balm.
Beneath the silvery boughs you'll find,
The fluttering secrets left behind.

# The Realm Beyond the Ferns' Gaze

Beyond the fronds where shadows play,
A hidden realm calls out to stray.
In ferns that whisper of the past,
A glimpse of time, a spell is cast.

Through tangled paths, the stories bloom,
Where light and shade create their room.
With every rustle, magic spins,
In realms where every heart begins.

The gentle creek sings lullabies,
As twilight settles, softly sighs.
A flicker bright, a voice so sweet,
Encourages lost souls to meet.

So take a step, your heart be brave,
In lands where dreams and hope can wave.
With every breath, the earth takes hold,
A promise etched in tales retold.

The realm awaits, a haven pure,
With every glance, the heart's allure.
So venture forth, let wonder blaze,
In magic found beyond the gaze.

# A Symphony of Lost Wishes

In twilight's reach, a tune unfolds,
A symphony of wishes told.
Each note a dream that slipped away,
In shadows cast by fading day.

With every sigh, a wish takes flight,
To dance among the stars so bright.
In echoes soft, their voices blend,
A call of hope that will not end.

Through every heart that bears the weight,
A melody begins to sate.
The laughter lost, the love once near,
Resonates in whispers clear.

So listen close, for you may hear,
The stories of the ones held dear.
A tapestry of dreams and tears,
Woven through the passing years.

A gentle breeze calls forth the past,
Where every wish is meant to last.
In every strum, the echo grows,
Of hopes and dreams the heart bestows.

Embrace the sound, let spirits fly,
For in this symphony, we try.
To reclaim what the heart once wished,
In melodies of love, unmissed.

# Whispers in the Glade

In twilight's hush, the secrets sigh,
As fireflies twinkle and stars draw nigh.
The trees lean close, in shadows they weave,
Ancient stories of those who believe.

Beneath the boughs, where dreams take flight,
A gentle breeze stirs, soft and light.
Laughter echoes, like a distant song,
Calling the heart where it truly belongs.

Moss carpeted paths, where footsteps tread,
With every stride, the night gently spreads.
The scent of pine, the cool, damp earth,
In this sacred space, we find our worth.

Oh, whispering leaves, share your tale,
Of love and magic that will not pale.
In the glade's embrace, we lose our fears,
And dance with the shadows that bring us cheer.

So linger a while in this enchanted place,
Where time stands still and hearts embrace.
In nature's cradle, we find our grace,
As the glade's whispers create a warm space.

# Enchantment's Silver Veil

Beneath the moon's soft, silver glow,
A whisper of magic begins to flow.
Through gossamer threads, the night unfolds,
With tales of wonder, softly retold.

The brook sings sweetly of distant lands,
While dew-kissed petals weave timeless strands.
Each shadow dances in the gentle night,
Wrapped in secrets, bathed in light.

Stars twinkle bright, like gems in the dark,
Illuminating dreams that dare to spark.
The air is thick with forgotten lore,
Inviting the heart to explore more.

A silver veil cloaks the world in dreams,
Awakening hope with its silken seams.
Every rustling leaf, every sighing tree,
Holds an enchantment, wild and free.

So wander beneath this mystical sky,
Let your soul soar, let your spirit fly.
For in this night, where wonders prevail,
Life dances lightly in enchantment's veil.

## Shadows Dance on Meadow Mists

In the quiet morn, where shadows play,
Whispers of mist begin to sway.
Dancing lightly on the cool, damp grass,
The day unfolds, as moments pass.

Sunlight breaks through, like a gentle kiss,
Waking the earth with a touch of bliss.
The flowers nod, in the fresh, dew-laden air,
A symphony born from nature's care.

With each soft step, the meadow sighs,
As butterflies flit, painting the skies.
The brook babbles secrets to the trees,
In this tranquil realm, the heart finds ease.

Shadows weave tales, soft and profound,
In the playful breeze, enchantments abound.
A tapestry stitched with threads of the day,
Crafting memories that never decay.

So linger a while, let the stillness fill,
As wonder awakens, and spirits thrill.
In the dance of shadows, let your heart roam,
In the meadow's embrace, you're always home.

# Lullabies of the Moonlit Grove

In the still of night, where magic brews,
The moon whispers softly to the dew.
Beneath the boughs, the world fades away,
As stars softly twinkle, in grand array.

Crickets serenade with a gentle hum,
While the forest stirs, and the night sings dumb.
Each leaf rustles softly, a calming refrain,
In the grove's lullaby, peace reigns.

Fireflies dance in a silken flight,
Guiding dreamers through the velvet night.
With every flicker, a wish takes wing,
In the hush of the grove, we learn to sing.

Night blooms unfold, their petals bright,
Releasing fragrances, sweet and light.
An ethereal balm for the weary soul,
In the moonlit grove, we find our whole.

So, rest your head 'neath the celestial dome,
Let the lullabies lead you softly home.
For here in the grove, life's mysteries sway,
Whispering dreams that never stray.

# Elusive Traces of Starlight's Dance

In the velvet night sky bright,
Whispers of stars twinkle light.
Dreams weave through the cosmic sea,
Traces of magic, wild and free.

Glimmers of tales yet untold,
Crafting shadows, silent and bold.
Each flicker a secret embrace,
A dance in the vastness of space.

The moon hums a silvery tune,
Guiding hearts to the night's boon.
With every sigh of the breeze,
Hopes ascend like fireflies with ease.

Among the clouds, echoes play,
Promises of a new dawn's sway.
Chasing the echoes of light,
Finding a path through the night.

Elusive traces, softly found,
In every corner, joy is bound.
For the stars hold a gentle glance,
Inviting us to join the dance.

## Fables in the Shade of Ancient Oaks

Beneath the canopy so grand,
Whispers linger, tales they hand.
History wrapped in rustling leaves,
In every corner, magic weaves.

Gnarled roots tell of times gone by,
In shadows deep, dreams fly high.
Each ring speaks of seasons passed,
Fables of ages, forever cast.

The breeze carries a soft caress,
Secrets of nature's sweet finesse.
From the ground to the highest bend,
Every branch holds a story, a friend.

In the dappled light, children roam,
Imaginations find their home.
With every step, adventures sprout,
Fables whispered, a gentle shout.

Gather round, for tales awake,
Each moment cherished, never fake.
In the shade of oaks, we find,
The magic that lives in heart and mind.

## Secrets in the Charmed Underbrush

In the undergrowth, shadows sway,
Secrets flourish in quaint array.
Whispers of life, soft and true,
Hidden wonders, waiting for you.

Moss carpets the earth like a dream,
Glimmers of gold in the sunbeam.
Every rustle, a gentle nudge,
Nature's pulse, we dare not judge.

Tiny creatures dance in delight,
Their world a puzzle, pure and bright.
Unseen magic in the small things,
In every flutter, a song that sings.

The air buzzes with stories spun,
Of sunlit days and moonlit run.
Costumed in green, deep and lush,
Secrets nestle in every hush.

Venture forth where shadows blend,
Among the ferns, let spirits mend.
For in the underbrush, we find,
The charm of nature, intertwined.

# The Enchantment of the Luminous Night

When twilight falls with a soft sigh,
Stars awaken, a twinkling sky.
The world transforms to a feast,
With night's soft touch, beauty released.

Under the glow of the moon's grace,
Shadows dance in a wondrous space.
Magic ripples through the air,
Promises linger, sweet and rare.

Owls call from the canopy high,
In mystical realms where dreams lie.
Every flicker of light inspires,
Fueling the heart with untamed fires.

Veils of silver and shades of blue,
Enchantment whispers, calling you.
The night is alive with tales to tell,
In the depths of darkness, all is well.

So linger long in this embrace,
Let starlit visions run their race.
For in the night, we find our way,
With every heartbeat, come what may.

# Echoes of Enchantment Through the Willows

In the quiet glade where shadows play,
Whispers of magic dance and sway.
Beneath the willows, secrets gleam,
Echoes of an ancient dream.

Moonlight weaves through branches wide,
A lantern's glow where dreams abide.
Sapphire streams with silver foam,
Guide the lost ones softly home.

Laughter lingers on the breeze,
Carried forth by rustling leaves.
Fables whispered, tales retold,
In twilight's grasp, our hearts unfold.

Glimmering dew on petals bright,
Painting dawn with hues of light.
A canvas stretched across the sky,
Where wishes take their wings and fly.

So wander close, don't stray too far,
For magic lives where wonders are.
In every rustle, in every sigh,
Echoes of enchantment never die.

# The Bloom of Wonder Under the Stars

Beneath the stars, in velvet night,
Dreams awaken, pure and bright.
Petals glowing in moon's soft kiss,
Whispers hint at magic's bliss.

Fires flicker in the cool night air,
Promises echo everywhere.
In gardens where wild secrets lay,
Children of wonder laugh and play.

Each bloom a tale of ages past,
Stories linger, shadows cast.
In every color, joy displayed,
The bloom of wonder, unafraid.

From twinkling skies to earth below,
The magic weaves a gentle flow.
With every heartbeat, every sigh,
Nature's wonders never die.

So gaze upon the starry sea,
And let your heart be wild and free.
For in this space, the world is bold,
The bloom of wonder to behold.

# Tread Lightly on Faery's Path

In glades where sunlight softly spills,
A hidden path through ancient hills.
Step lightly, friend, with gentle grace,
For faery magic fills this place.

Mossy stones and fragrant blooms,
Awake in night's enchanting gloom.
Crickets sing their twilight song,
Inviting all to linger long.

With every step, a secret shared,
Stories woven, gently dared.
In the hush, the faeries dance,
A world alive with sweet romance.

Sparkling lights like fireflies,
Glide through shadows, soft and wise.
Hold your breath, let silence reign,
For whispers linger in the grain.

So tread lightly on this path divine,
Where dreams and daylight intertwine.
In faery realms, let your heart soar,
Embrace the magic, seek for more.

# Woven Whispers of the Glade

In the heart of the whispering wood,
Where the ancients once understood,
Woven tales in the evening light,
Softly beckon, a lovely sight.

Nestled in the ferns so green,
Hidden wonders wait unseen.
Breeze carries songs of yesteryear,
Charming echoes drawing near.

Gentle twilight wraps the trees,
In every rustle, secrets flee.
The stars confide in shadows bold,
Stories whispered, treasures told.

When night descends and dreams arise,
The glade unveils its secret skies.
In hushed reverence, spirits dance,
Entwined in night's soft, sweet romance.

So wander forth in moonlit grace,
And let enchantment find its place.
For woven whispers softly play,
In the magic of the glade, we stay.

# Luminous Shadows of the Woodland

In the heart of the grove, where the wildflowers sway,
Luminous shadows dance at the end of the day.
Whispers of magic drift on the breeze,
Tales of enchantment that urge us to seize.

Crimson and gold in the fading light,
Secrets awaken with the fall of the night.
Beneath ancient boughs with their gnarled embrace,
The woodland of dreams holds a mystical space.

Footsteps are whispered, yet never alone,
Creatures and spirits in harmony's tone.
Branches above weave a tapestry deep,
Guardians of wonder, their vigil they keep.

Stars blink awake as the night claims the sky,
Casting a glow on the world passing by.
Leaves sing with laughter, the wood's gentle hum,
While shadows play games, as if beckoning fun.

With hearts full of joy and eyes wide with glee,
We wander amid what the forest can be.
In luminous shadows, our spirits will soar,
Embraced by the magic forever, once more.

## Dreams Drenched in Twilight's Gaze

When twilight descends on the edge of the night,
Dreams drench the valley in soft, silver light.
Stars bathe the world in a shimmering glow,
Inviting the wanderers where wishes can flow.

A river of thoughts in velvety streams,
Cradled by silence, where softly it beams.
In the quietest corners of slumbering earth,
Mysteries linger, waiting for birth.

Time weaves a tapestry, gentle and fine,
Threads of the cosmic, twisting in line.
Colors of hope in each shadowed embrace,
Illuminating joys in this still, sacred space.

As visions take flight in the soft waning light,
Dreams draped in stardust take wing, taking flight.
The art of the night dances close to our hearts,
Awakening wonders as daylight departs.

In the hush of the dusk, as the world holds its breath,
We find a connection that dances with depth.
With dreams drenched in twilight, we enter a phase,
A symphony woven in twilight's gaze.

# Fantasies Wrapped in Gossamer Threads

In the realm of the fanciful where day meets the night,
Fantasies flourish in shimmer and light.
Gossamer threads weave the tales of our hearts,
Binding together the world with fine arts.

Each whisper is colored in magical hues,
Stories unlock as the dreamers infuse.
Bouncing on starlight, they skip through the air,
With laughter and wonder, all spirits laid bare.

Secrets entwined in each silvery strand,
Holding the whispers of a faraway land.
Crafted with care, the enchantments arise,
Mirroring starlight that dances in eyes.

In realms where the fanciful take gentle flight,
Every heartbeat becomes a soft, glowing light.
Awakening visions like blooms in the spring,
Fantasies beckon—oh, the joy they can bring!

As twilight unfurls her delicate lace,
We bathe in the magic of such wondrous grace.
Wrapped in those threads, ever softly we tread,
Lost in the dreams that vividly spread.

# Elfin Lullabies on the Wind

Softly they sing in the twilight's embrace,
Elfin lullabies drifting with grace.
Carried on breezes from glen to the vale,
Whispers of magic where fairies prevail.

In shadows that dance, beneath moon's gentle beam,
Each note is a promise, each melody, a dream.
Ethereal voices wrapped snugly in night,
Cradle the stars in the silvery light.

Flutes made of petals and harps of pure dew,
Play tunes of the forest as if they are new.
Calling the wanderers, inviting the lost,
To savor the sweetness of dreams that exhaust.

As laughter flutters in the cool evening air,
Elfin charms linger in whispers of care.
Secured in the silence of shadows that twine,
Beauty surrounds us, forever divine.

With every soft sigh, our hearts learn to listen,
To elfin lullabies, where the starlight will glisten.
The magic of night weaves a blanket of peace,
As dreams glide like visions, and troubles release.

# Threads of the Ethereal Whisper

In twilight's grasp, the stars align,
Soft whispers weave through the vine.
A tapestry of dreams takes flight,
While shadows dance in the waning light.

Each thread a story, spun with care,
Echoes of laughter fill the air.
Magic swirls in the gentle breeze,
Unraveling secrets beneath the trees.

In every flutter, a heartbeat sings,
The past entwined with forgotten things.
A sigh of fate in the cool night air,
Threads of the ethereal, beyond compare.

The moonlight glimmers, casting spells,
In whispered tones, a tale compels.
Softly, softly, the night unfolds,
A world where wonder's light beholds.

And as the dawn begins to break,
The whispers fade, with dreams to wake.
Yet in our hearts, they softly stay,
Threads of magic, never fray.

## Chasing Shadows of the Ancient Spring

Beneath the boughs where whispers cling,
We chase the shadows of ancient spring.
With every step on mossy ground,
Echoes of laughter softly found.

The river's song, a gentle hum,
Calls forth the creatures, many come.
In vibrant blooms of colors bright,
The world awakens to morning light.

A flicker here, a rustle there,
The forest breathes a fragrant air.
Each winding path a tale unfurl,
As petals dance and soft winds whirl.

In this embrace, we share our dreams,
Beneath the sun's warm, golden beams.
With every heartbeat, nature sings,
Chasing shadows of ancient springs.

As twilight whispers, shadows creep,
We carry memories, ours to keep.
With every heartbeat, time takes wing,
Chasing shadows through wandering spring.

# Serenade of Luminous Leaves

In golden hues, the leaves take flight,
Dancing softly in the fading light.
A serenade of rustling sounds,
As autumn's breath paints all around.

Each leaf a note, a story spun,
In vibrant hues beneath the sun.
Whispers carried on the gentle breeze,
Luminous leaves bring hearts to ease.

Through twisted roots and branches bare,
A melody hums, filling the air.
In every flutter, a moment caught,
A fleeting glimpse of wonder sought.

The winds sing secrets from days of yore,
As nature's song unlocks her door.
With every rustle, a tale bestowed,
Serenade of leaves along the road.

And as the dusk paints skies in gold,
The stories weave, forever told.
In dreams, we roam where whispers gleave,
To dance once more with luminous leaves.

# Tales Unspooled Beneath the Faery Dance

Amidst the glen where shadows play,
Tales unspool in a magical way.
With every twirl, the faeries prance,
Weaving joy in a merry dance.

Dance of the stars, glimmers so bright,
In the embrace of the soft moonlight.
Enchanting laughter fills the air,
As tales unfurl, light as a prayer.

Secrets of old in whispers shared,
The night alive, with dreams prepared.
In every flicker of gentle glow,
The heart of the forest begins to show.

Around the fire, stories ignite,
Of worlds unseen, lost to the night.
With every sparkle, a tale divine,
Beneath the faery dance, we entwine.

And as dawn's blush begins to rise,
The magic lingers, never dies.
In dreams we weave, as shadows prance,
Tales unspooled in the faery dance.

## The Gathering of Fern and Spell

In the glade where magic twirls,
The ferns whisper ancient songs,
Beneath the moon, the forest swirls,
Casting spells where beauty throngs.

Crickets sing as stars ignite,
A gathering of hidden kin,
In shadowed glen, a sacred rite,
Where wonders weave and dreams begin.

Softly glows the night's embrace,
With fireflies dancing in delight,
Laughter echoes through the space,
A tapestry of purest light.

Secrets shared through whispered breath,
As shadows meld and merge with grace,
Each moment cherished, life from death,
In this enchanted, timeless place.

# Twilight's Faery Reverie

In twilight's glow, where faeries play,
With laughter sweet as summer's rain,
They dance upon the fading day,
In realms untouched by sorrow's stain.

Soft petals fall in swirling flight,
Glimmering as the stars awake,
With shimmered wings they take their height,
In dreams that twilight's breath shall make.

The moon bestows her silver sheen,
As whispers float on evening's air,
A world of wonder, soft and green,
Where magic thrives without a care.

Through sylvan paths and moss-clad stones,
They weave the night with gentle mirth,
In twilight's arms, they find their homes,
A faery reverie of earth.

## Secrets Wrapped in Gossamer

In dusk-filled corners, shadows play,
With secrets wrapped in gossamer,
A tale emerges, soft and fey,
Of whispers lost and dreams that stir.

The air is thick with magic's song,
As twilight beckons, spells awaken,
In hidden realms where heartbeats throng,
And every silence feels unshaken.

Enchanted threads of silver spin,
Translucent veils of twilight's breath,
Within their folds, where wonders grin,
Lies the delicate dance of death.

So tiptoe softly, heed the call,
Through veils of night, let courage lead,
For in this realm where shadows fall,
Secrets of dreams and truth shall seed.

# Dance of the Shimmering Shadows

In the moonlight's soft caress,
Shadows gather, poised to play,
Their shimmering forms, a wild mess,
At the threshold of night and day.

With twinkling eyes and laughter bright,
They sway to the rhythm of the breeze,
A dance that flares in silver light,
Entwined beneath the ancient trees.

Whispers carry through the air,
Of secrets shared in timeless peace,
Every flicker, a tale laid bare,
As shadows shiver, and then release.

So come, dear friend, join in the fun,
Let your spirit loose and wild,
For in this dance, we are all one,
A shimmering joy, forever styled.

# Secrets of the Dreamwells Unseen

In shadows deep where whispers dwell,
The secrets lie in a woven spell.
A flicker bright, a glimpse of light,
In dreamwells hidden from our sight.

The moonlight dances on water's seam,
Carrying tales from a silent dream.
A heart that listens, a soul that knows,
Unlocks the path where mystery flows.

In every corner, enchantments weave,
Stories waiting, if we believe.
The stars above act as key and guide,
To realms where forgotten hopes reside.

With each soft sigh, the shadows play,
Chasing the dreams that drift away.
In the hushed hush of night's embrace,
The hidden truths reveal their grace.

So dip your toes in the twilight stream,
And find the magic in every dream.
For in the well where the secrets flow,
Lies the essence of all we long to know.

# The Solitude of Wandering Spirits

In the stillness of the evening haze,
Wandering spirits weave their ways.
Through ancient woods where shadows sigh,
They linger softly, passing by.

Each rustling leaf, each whispering breeze,
Carries secrets among the trees.
The echoes of what once was bright,
Fading gently into the night.

Beneath the stars, they gently roam,
Searching for a place called home.
With silent steps, they trace the ground,
In solitude their peace is found.

Though unseen, their presence glows,
In every heart where longing flows.
A tapestry of lost desires,
Woven softly with unseen fires.

In twilight's grasp, their whispers weave,
Tales of love that never leave.
For in the silence, bonds remain,
Wandering spirits dance through pain.

# Phantoms Beneath the Old Oak

Beneath the branches, gnarled and wise,
Phantoms gather 'neath twilight skies.
With stories etched in bark and stone,
They cradle dreams of those long gone.

In flickering light of fireflies' glow,
Ancient murmurs rise and flow.
The old oak watches with patient grace,
As memories drift in a timeless space.

With every sigh of swirling breeze,
Phantoms laugh and speak with ease.
Their laughter resonates through the night,
Echoes of joy, pure delight.

Yet sorrow clings to each faint wisp,
A bittersweet grasp, a tender lisp.
In shadows deep, their tales entwine,
Holding close what once was mine.

So pause awhile, beneath the oak,
Listen closely to every joke.
For in those phantoms, love abides,
And in their whispers, the heart resides.

# A Melody of Forgotten Dreams

In a secret glade where the wildflowers sway,
Whispers of dreams from yesterday play.
A melody swirls in the crisp, cool air,
Echoes of wishes still floating there.

With each gentle breeze, a tune takes flight,
Carrying hopes into the night.
Every note a story, a memory spun,
A tapestry woven in laughter and fun.

The past and present entwined so tight,
In the soft hum of fading light.
With every sigh, a heart recalls,
The laughter, the moments, the silent falls.

In this symphony of seasons lost,
Beauty breathes, though we pay the cost.
For dreams once cherished may fade away,
Yet their melody forever will stay.

So listen close, let the music seep,
Into the corners, where shadows creep.
In forgotten dreams, where magic gleams,
Lies a melody for the heart's quiet themes.

## Glimmers of Starlight in the Thicket

In the thicket where shadows play,
Glimmers of starlight dance and sway.
Whispers of night, in the cool, soft air,
Guide weary travelers with gentle care.

Moss carpets pathways, ancient and wise,
Each step unveils a world in disguise.
The moon casts secrets through branches wide,
Where dreams and enchantments quietly bide.

Silver leaves shimmer, a fragile spell,
Echoes of laughter, a distant bell.
Creatures of twilight awaken their night,
In hidden realms bathed in soft, gentle light.

Fireflies flicker, like wishes on wings,
Illuminating the hopes that it brings.
The thicket is alive with stories untold,
A tapestry woven in silver and gold.

So linger a moment, let time slip away,
In the glow of the thicket, let your heart stay.
For forgotten magic in shadows does weave,
And glimmers of starlight are all you believe.

# The Veil Between Worlds Unraveled

Beyond the mist where the worlds entwine,
Lies a veil of magic, both fragile and fine.
With a whisper of breath, it shimmers and shakes,
A passage to wonder, where silence awakes.

Footsteps echo on the soft, mossy floor,
As shadows embrace each enchanted door.
The air is alive with a soft, knowing hum,
Inviting the lost and the curious to come.

Night creatures gather, their eyes burn like coals,
Guardians of secrets, keepers of souls.
Through ribbons of light, they beckon and sway,
To reimagine the dawn of a different day.

Glimpses of realms where the wild whispers play,
Where clouds weave tales in a fanciful way.
The veil quivers softly, as if to confess,
That magic is waiting, a timeless caress.

So tread lightly, dear hearts, through the shrouded
expanse,
Where one's wildest dreams leap and twirl in a dance.
For the veil between worlds, once thought to be tight,
Is a gossamer thread spun from the fabric of night.

# Nightfall's Caress in the Ferny Nook

In a ferny nook where the shadows blend,
Nightfall descends, a soft, gentle friend.
With a melody hushed, it wraps the land,
In dreams woven fine by a silvery hand.

Stars twinkle bright, like the eyes of the wise,
Guardians of secrets that slumber and rise.
Each whisper of wind tells a tale long ago,
Of magic and mystery only night knows.

Crickets sing softly, a lullaby sweet,
As pathways of starlight beneath our feet greet.
The moon hangs low, a vigilant guide,
Lending its light to the wanderers' stride.

Shadows dance gently, in elegant twirls,
While fern fronds unfurl, like delicate pearls.
Numbers of night creatures sing a soft tune,
Beneath the warm glow of the watchful moon.

So linger a while, in this haven of peace,
With nightfall's caress, let your worries cease.
For in the ferny nook where enchantments call,
You'll find that the shadows embrace one and all.

# Murmurs of Forgotten Legends

In the heart of the woods where the old tales dwell,
Murmurs of legends weave their magic spell.
Whispers in breezes, soft stories untold,
Awakening echoes of heroes of old.

Branches entwined like the fates of the brave,
Guardians of knowledge, their secrets they save.
Each rustle and sigh speaks of battle and glory,
A tapestry rich in a long-forgotten story.

Sparkling laughs flutter like leaves in the air,
An invocation of spirits laid bare.
Through twilight's embrace, they share their regret,
A longing for memories, timeless and set.

With candlelight glimmering, the past comes alive,
And the pulse of the unknown begins to revive.
A chorus of voices resounds through the night,
In the dance of the shadows, an ethereal sight.

So pause for a moment, and listen, take heed,
For the murmurs of legends plant magical seed.
In the hush of the forest, where memories blend,
The stories will carry, and never will end.

## Dances of Fireflies at Dusk

In the soft embrace of twilight glow,
Fireflies twinkle with a gentle show.
They waltz through whispers, secrets they keep,
In the meadow where shadows and silence leap.

A flicker of magic, a dance in the air,
Spinner of dreams, they glide without care.
Each spark ignites wonder, a story untold,
In the cool of the evening, where night takes hold.

With laughter of nightingales rising in song,
They spiral and twirl, where moments belong.
Beneath the fading sun, in the dimming light,
A symphony twirls in the calm of the night.

The brush of their wings, like whispers of fate,
Entwined with the dusk as the world waits.
In the heart of enchantment, they flicker and soar,
Guiding us gently to magic's sweet door.

So linger a while, let the wonder unfold,
In dances of fireflies, stories retold.
For when dusk settles soft, and dreams intertwine,
We find in their glow the light of the divine.

# The Tapestry of Chiara's Dreams

In the quiet hours when the stars convene,
Chiara weaves visions, bright and serene.
Threads of her hopes, shimmering and bright,
A tapestry crafted in the softest light.

With colors of moonbeams and whispers of night,
She knots each memory, taking flight.
A splash of adventure, a dash of delight,
In the loom of her heart, her dreams take their height.

As dawn's first blush brushes the sky,
She gathers the stories that dance and fly.
Each thread tells a tale, both vibrant and true,
Of castles and kingdoms tucked under the blue.

From mountains of stardust to rivers of gold,
Her tapestry shimmers, each piece a strong hold.
With every connection of laughter and tear,
She weaves the extraordinary, bright and clear.

So cherish her dreams, let them float and gleam,
In the tapestry woven by Chiara's dream.
For within every thread, a wondrous refrain,
Is the heartbeat of magic, unbroken by pain.

# Capricious Breezes in Hidden Glens

In a glen where shadows twist and sway,
Capricious breezes dance and play.
They whisper secrets only trees can hear,
Carrying tales of joy and fear.

Through the ferns and moss, they twirl so free,
Kissing the petals of a wild magnolia tree.
With a gentle touch, they stir the serene,
Painting the leaves in strokes so keen.

They waltz with the daisies, weave through the grass,
A playful reminder of moments that pass.
Each puff of wind holds a memory dear,
Of laughter and love that linger near.

In the hush of the glen, they spiral and swirl,
Inviting the dreams of each boy and girl.
They carry the essence of stories untold,
In the heart of the forest, where magic unfolds.

So listen closely when the breezes breathe,
For the tales of the glens are treasures to weave.
In the dance of the winds, feel the joy they send,
In their capricious laughter, let your heart mend.

# Luminous Secrets of the Twilight Realm

As twilight dances on the edge of the night,
The realm awakens, bathed in soft light.
Luminous secrets unfurl in the air,
Whispering stories that only we share.

Each glimmering star tells a wish long gone,
With echoes of laughter, a mystical song.
In the shadows, a flicker, a glint from afar,
Holds the promise of dreams, like a distant star.

The moon spills silver, casting wishes that flow,
In the heart of the night, where wonders grow.
Amidst the ethereal glow, we find our way,
Chasing the secrets that twilight will say.

With the rustle of leaves and the sigh of the breeze,
The twilight realm whispers, inviting us to seize.
Every heartbeat synchronized with the night,
Ignites the magic hidden from sight.

So wander these realms until dawn's break,
For in luminous secrets, the heart will awake.
In the glow of the twilight, let your spirit roam,
Discover your magic, and call it home.

## Whispering Leaves of the Lost Valley

In twilight's glow, the shadows creep,
Where secrets murmur, dark and deep.
A breeze that sighs through ancient trees,
Holds stories lost on whispered knees.

The petals flutter, soft and bright,
Dancing gently in the light.
Each rustling leaf a tale to tell,
Of dreams and sorrows, magic's spell.

Beneath the boughs of emerald shade,
Memories linger, never fade.
A place where time is slow and sweet,
And every heartbeat skips a beat.

With every step on winding paths,
The spirit stirs, and laughter lasts.
In twilight's web, enchantments weave,
The world awakens, and we believe.

So lose yourself in twilight's grace,
Embrace the dream, a soft embrace.
For in this vale, where echoes lie,
The lost will linger, never die.

## Beneath Canopies of Emerald Whisper

Beneath the leaves, the shadows play,
Where sunlight dances, bright and gay.
A world awakens, wild and free,
In emerald whispers, tales to see.

The glens are rich with fragrant bloom,
Drawing forth a sweet perfume.
With every rustle, stories twine,
As spirits weave in sacred rhyme.

Look closely now, the fairies glide,
On shimmering wings, they slip and slide.
Their laughter echoes, pure delight,
As day transforms to dazzling night.

In every nook, a magic spark,
As shadows stretch from light to dark.
With every heartbeat, time concedes,
To mysteries lost among the leaves.

So wander deep where wonders bloom,
And let your heart lift from its gloom.
Beneath the boughs that whisper cheer,
A world of dreams forever near.

## Charms of the Forgotten Fairies

In hidden glades where time stands still,
The fairies weave with gentle will.
On silver threads of moonlight's hue,
They spin enchanting tales anew.

With petals soft as morning dew,
They craft their spells both bright and true.
A flicker here, a shimmer there,
Their laughter floats upon the air.

Each charm they cast, a twinkling light,
Infuses dreams that dance in flight.
In twilight's magic, wishes wait,
For hearts to dare and contemplate.

Among the ferns, the whispers play,
Of love and joy, both night and day.
In secret corners, find the glee,
Of charms entwined with destiny.

So heed the call, look deep inside,
For where the fairies flit and bide,
The past and future gently meet,
In joyous rhythm, bittersweet.

# Echoing Steps in the Phantom Woods

In phantom woods, the echoes call,
Where shadows lengthen, rise, and fall.
With every step, the whispers sigh,
And time's embrace moves softly by.

A pathway lost, yet never gone,
With secrets held until the dawn.
The trees, they lean with ancient weight,
To listen close, to hold our fate.

The moonbeams dance on silvered bark,
Lighting paths that lead through dark.
Each rustling branch, a voice declared,
A story spun, for those who dared.

The nightingale sings soft and low,
A haunting tune from long ago.
In every heartbeat, tales repeat,
Of dreams and fears, in shadows meet.

So tread the paths where echoes meet,
With cautious heart and steady feet.
For in the woods, where phantoms dwell,
Lies magic we can yet compel.

## Enigmatic Glimmers in the Dusk

In the twilight's tender light,
Shadows dance, taking flight.
Whispers echo through the trees,
Carried softly by the breeze.

Stars awaken, shyly glow,
Secrets hidden, hearts aglow.
Each flicker tells a tale anew,
Of dreams spun in midnight's brew.

Moonbeams paint the silent ground,
Every rustle, a mystic sound.
Glimmers burst, like laughter bright,
In the embrace of gentle night.

Daylight fades, and silence grows,
In the dark, a soft wind blows.
Through the veil of dusk we tread,
Following paths the stars have spread.

The world transforms, a wondrous sight,
In the fusion of day and night.
Enigmatic glimmers guide our way,
Until we greet the dawn's first ray.

## The Allure of Fern-Cloaked Secrets

In the forest, shadows play,
Where ferns in green hues sway.
Beneath their leaves, tales reside,
Of creatures that in dreams abide.

Misty paths weave through the glade,
Veils of fog, a transient shade.
Each step whispers a secret lore,
Enticing souls to wander more.

Twisting branches, time-worn bark,
Hold the stories bright and dark.
In the stillness of the noon,
A lullaby of nature's tune.

Breezes carry scents of old,
Where the tales of magic unfold.
Fern-cloaked secrets, sweet and rare,
Are woven through the fragrant air.

To seek the truth in leafy shades,
Where mystery, in silence, invades.
The whispers draw me ever near,
Ever hidden, yet so clear.

# Fragments of Long-Lost Dreams

In the corners of the mind,
Echoes of dreams we left behind.
Scattered like leaves in autumn's chase,
Each memory holds a soft embrace.

Through time's fingers, moments slip,
Vanishing like a fleeting ship.
Yet in the dark, they spark and gleam,
Whispers of long-lost, yearning dream.

Fanciful worlds of joy and light,
Haunt the quiet hours of night.
Fragments float on twilight's breath,
Reminders of what love bequeaths.

They beckon softly, urging flight,
To fill the heart with pure delight.
In every sigh, a story sewn,
The threads of dreams we once had known.

As dawn unfolds with golden hue,
Awakening the dreamers' view.
We gather shards, and piece by piece,
Revive the dreams that never cease.

## Revelations in the Twilight Mist

Veils of mist shroud the night,
Secrets born of silver light.
In the haze, the world feels new,
Whispers call, out of the blue.

Every shadow hides a clue,
Things unseen, yet felt so true.
As the stars begin to wake,
Glimmers rise from the still lake.

Thoughts like birds in flight take wing,
Hopes and fears, a fragile string.
Caught in the twilight's soft embrace,
Life unfolds with gentle grace.

In this hour, all is revealed,
Hidden truths that fate concealed.
Grasp the light, let go of fear,
In the mist, all becomes clear.

The heart knows what the mind can't see,
In twilight's dance, we all are free.
With every breath, a dream ignites,
Revelations of endless nights.

www.ingramcontent.com/pod-product-compliance
Ingram Content Group UK Ltd.
Pitfield, Milton Keynes, MK11 3LW, UK
UKHW021317280125
4330UKWH00005B/295